2 INTRODUCTION

4 CANADA: THE OTHER AR...
A young man aged 75
Conscription or voluntary service? — 4
From wood pulp to tanks — 7

8 PREPARING FOR D-DAY
Dieppe: a tragic lesson — 8
Overlord and the 3rd Canadian Division — 10
The Atlantic Wall on Juno Beach — 14

16 JUNO BEACH, A GATEWAY TO THE FORTRESS EUROPE
D-Day on Juno Beach — 16
  07:49 The Royal Winnipeg Rifles land to the west of the River Seulles
  08:00 The North Shore (New Brunswick) Regiment lands in Saint-Aubin
  08:05 The Regina Rifles attack WN 29 at Courseulles
  08:00 The Queen's Own Rifles of Canada struggle in Bernières
Inland progression — 23
Progressive disillusionment — 25
The liberation of the rest of Europe — 30

32 JUNO BEACH TODAY

OREP
EDITIONS

15, rue de Largerie 14480 CULLY
Tel. 02 31 08 31 08 - Fax 02 31 08 31 09
info@orep-pub.com - www.orep-pub.com

Editor: Philippe Pique
Editorial coordinator: Corine Desprez
English translation: Heather Costil

Graphic design: OREP
ISBN: 978-2-8151-0038-0 – © Éditions OREP 2010
All rights reserved – Legal deposit: 2nd quarter 2011

JUNO BEACH

Canadian soldiers in an LCA (Landing Craft Assault) barge. *National Archives of Canada - PA 132790.*

What can this young Canadian be thinking of, aboard his landing craft on the dawn of the 6th of June 1944? What can Yvon, Réjean or John be thinking of, so far from home?

Perhaps, indeed, his homeland, over 8,000 kilometres from here. The Manitoba lakes, the banks of the St. Lawrence River or the plains of Saskatchewan. Will he return there one day, to see the family he left behind over four years ago?

Is he sufficiently trained to survive what is in store for him? For over a year, he has been repeating the same manoeuvres. Will they help him not to fall on the beaches as his cousin, Colin, did in Dieppe? What traps have the Germans laid to prevent him from accomplishing his mission?

Then again, maybe he's thinking of nothing. Maybe he's just stopped thinking, overwhelmed by seasickness amidst these tumultuous waters. Soaked by the sea spray, he has but one wish: to finally set foot on French soil, on that sandy stretch of coast code named Juno Beach.

CANADA:
THE OTHER ARSENAL OF DEMOCRACY

A YOUNG MAN AGED 75

On the 10th of September 1939, Canada declared war against the German Reich, hence endorsing its commitment to the British Commonwealth. However, it was the last nation to do so. As such, it hoped to demonstrate its sovereignty as an independent State, whilst endeavouring to ensure that the French-speaking community take no umbrage. Indeed, in 1939, the new generation of French colonists continued to snub the British hegemony. Consequently, the nation's unity remained fragile.

At the beginning of the Second World War, Canada was but a young man aged 75. The British North America Acts that had reunited the provinces of Ontario, Quebec, New Brunswick and Nova Scotia only dated from 1867, the integration of the last two provinces, Saskatchewan and Alberta, being implemented later, in 1905. Canada's 9 provinces and 2 territories were, at the time, home to a contrasting population of over 11 million inhabitants. Contrasting for, whilst over 50% were of British and Irish origin, the country was also home to a vast French-speaking community, essentially in Quebec. German, Ukrainian and Dutch immigrants had also settled in Canada. Contrasting also, due to the fact that two thirds of the country's population lived exclusively in Ontario and Quebec.

The Canadian Prime Minister **William Lyon Mackenzie King** (1874-1950).
His first political post was as Deputy Minister of Labour in 1909, later to become leader of the Liberal Party in 1919. He was appointed Prime Minister in 1921, to be re-elected on several occasions up to 1948.

CONSCRIPTION OR VOLUNTARY SERVICE?

When war was declared, these Quebecers were delighted to hear the Prime Minister himself, William Lyon Mackenzie King, declare that he would never resort to conscription for overseas military service. Indeed, 1917, the year they had been forced into combat alongside their British counterparts, was still fresh in their memories. This situation had jeopardised the nation's unity, for the French-speaking community was averse to the idea of

The Canadians sent to fight in Europe were volunteers, contrary to the majority of other nations which reverted to conscription. *Juno Beach Centre.*

enlisting alongside its former enemy. The question of conscription was nevertheless to upset the political and social climate throughout the entire war, French Canadians striving to preserve their territorial liberty and refusing to extend their existing war effort, whilst the English-speaking community was looking for a more spirited commitment alongside Great Britain.

A referendum, organised on the 27th of April 1942, failed to solve the problem. To the somewhat obtuse question, "Are you in favour of releasing the government from any obligations arising out of any past commitments restricting the methods of raising men for military service?", 64% of the total population voted yes, whereas 72% of Quebecers voted no, upon which, the situation reached a dead end. However, the issue was to surface once more following great losses in 1944 in Italy and Normandy.

At the beginning of the war, Canada's army was limited to 8,000 men and its defence policy relied principally on protecting its American neighbours and British cousins. Voluntary service proved successful to such

Young Canadians enlisting in a military recruiting office in 1939. A total of over one million Canadians enlisted for voluntary service under the Canadian flag (45% of the 18-45 year age group).

Anti-conscription demonstration by students from the University of Montreal (March 1939). The majority of Quebecers remained opposed to conscription throughout the entire war. Their opposition was confirmed by referendum on the 27th of April 1942 with 72% of NO votes.

One last kiss before leaving for Halifax, where these men from the 2nd Division were to embark for Great Britain (July 1940). Will he see his sweetheart again?

National Archives of Canada - PA 114201.

an extent that around 45% of the male population aged from 18 to 45 was to serve under the Canadian flag, i.e. over a million voluntary servicemen. Canadian warships protected the Atlantic convoys, Canadian pilots took part in the Battle of Britain in 1940, whilst five divisions were posted on the other side of the Atlantic. However, voluntary service failed to compensate for the great losses sustained in Italy and Normandy. In November 1944, a contingent of 16,000 men in charge of defending the nation, all of them conscripts, enabled Canada's ranks to be sufficiently reinforced without causing major detriment to the nation's unity.

These women are checking 25-pound shell cartridges. As in many countries, with the exception of Germany, women compensated for the men absent on the front, by working in munitions plants. They were the Arsenal of Democracy's working hands.
National Archives of Canada - PA 112912.

▲ The Royal Canadian Air Force fought alongside the British during the Battle of Britain in July 1940. Several British pilots also trained in Canada as part of the British Commonwealth Air Training Plan. *Juno Beach Centre.*

FROM WOOD PULP TO TANKS

Over and above the conscription issue, the 1929 economic crisis had generated considerable tension between communities. Exportation of raw materials (wood, wheat...) or semi-finished products such as wood pulp, was on the decline to such an extent that, in 1939, the national revenue was even lower than in 1929, inevitably leading to an upsurge in unemployment which affected over 20% of the population.

Besides the provision of volunteer recruits, Canada turned to producing supplies to support Great Britain. As early as 1939, the country's economy was transformed into a war economy. Despite a slow start, Canada's industrial effort was to eventually prove substantial. Created almost from nothing, naval and aeronautical construction yards and munitions plants rapidly emerged, producing the weapons that were to supply Great Britain, at a time when the latter challenged, alone, the German threat. From an initial budget of $120 million in the early days of the war, Canada's defence budget reached $4.5 billion in 1944, i.e. 87% of total State expenditure. In barely five years, Canada had become, alongside the United States, the Arsenal of Democracy, producing around 900,000 vehicles of all sorts and over a million light weapons.

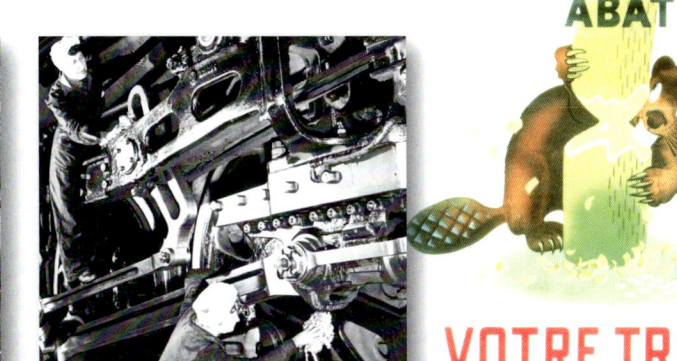

Propaganda poster. *Juno Beach Centre.*

▲ Canada produced essentially vehicles and light weapons. However, locomotives were also shipped across the Atlantic to supply the Allied armies throughout their progression. *National Archives of Canada - C 79525.*

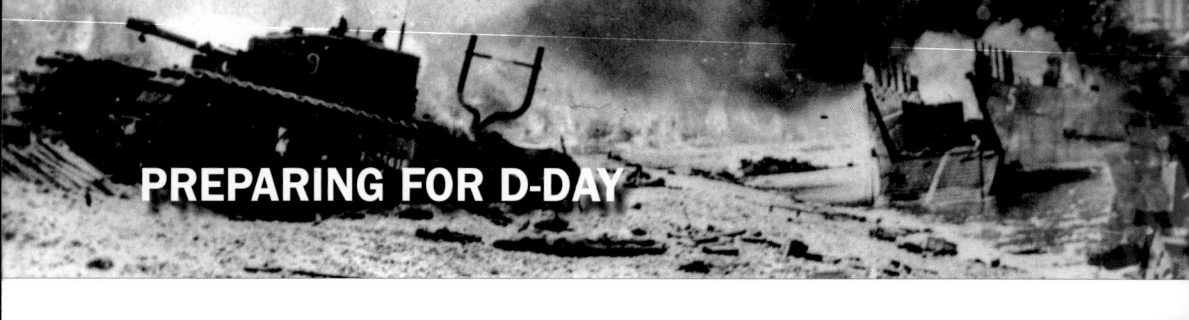

PREPARING FOR D-DAY

DIEPPE: A TRAGIC LESSON

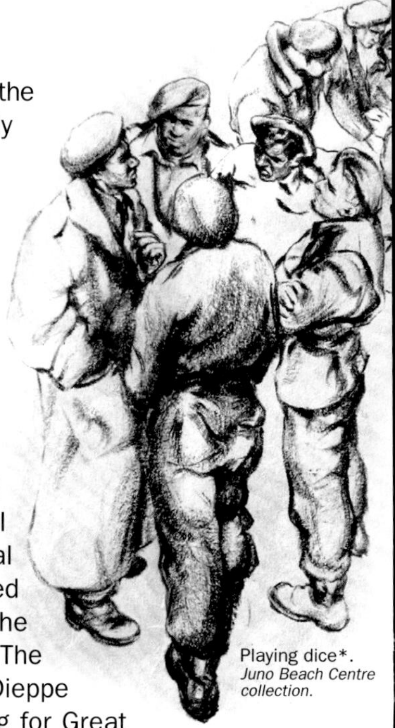

Playing dice*. *Juno Beach Centre collection.*

The first convoy of Canadian troops arrived in Great Britain on the 17th of December 1939. However, these men were insufficiently prepared for modern warfare. They were consequently trained in the vicinity of Aldershot before being sent to France in June 1940. Following disastrous developments on the French front, the Canadians re-embarked almost immediately.

The period that followed was relatively inactive and the Canadians were entrusted with defending the Sussex coast. Their training for the D-Day Landings began in September 1941.

The project to organise a major assault on the French coast, in order to test landing techniques, emerged in Lord Mountbatten's Combined Operations headquarters in April 1942. The strategists behind the operation, General Montgomery and Lord Mountbatten himself, rapidly entrusted the Canadians with the greater part of the mission, which they code named Jubilee. The aim was to take control of the port of Dieppe and its defences, before re-embarking for Great Britain. The mission was entrusted to the 2nd Canadian Division under General Roberts, reinforced by Churchill tanks from the Calgary Regiment. British commandos, along with a handful of American rangers also took part in the operation.

Hence, on the 18th of August, over 6,000 men, 4,963 of them Canadian, headed for the French coast. At 04:00 hours the following morning, they were geared up for combat. However, the welcome they were to receive from the 302nd German Division was hostile and proved to be fatal. The landing troops were massacred on Dieppe beach, whilst the Churchill tanks

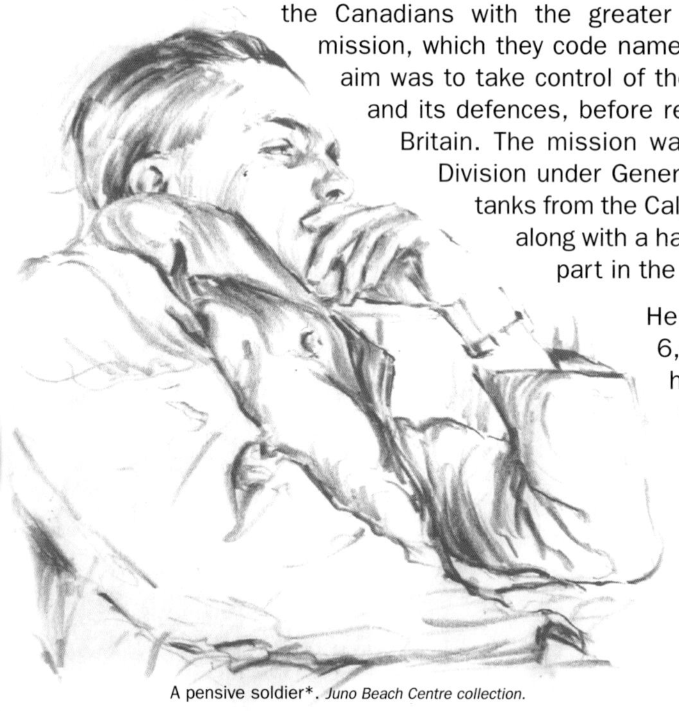

A pensive soldier*. *Juno Beach Centre collection.*

*Drawings by Jim Bardsley form the Canadian Forces Health Services.

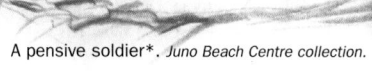

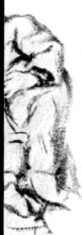

advanced at a snail's pace across the pebble stones. At 09:00 hours, they received orders to withdraw. The last men re-embarked four hours later. The Canadians had lost a total of 3,369 men, 900 of them killed and 1,944 taken prisoner.

However, although a bitter defeat, Operation Jubilee was to serve as a lesson at several levels. First of all, from a tactical point of view, it was now clear that the success of any landing operation would require excellent land-air-sea coordination. The Canadians consequently intensified training to that effect. Secondly, armoured support was essential. The beaches chosen needed to be suitable for their progression and new tanks needed to be developed, capable of triumphing over the beach defences set up by the Germans. General Percy Hobart set to the task with great success, creating an entire "menagerie" of anti-mine tanks, bridge building tanks, Churchill tanks equipped with Petard mortars, bunker destroyers and even amphibious Duplex Drive tanks.

Soldiers from the 2nd Division on their way back to England following the failed Operation Jubilee. Their uniforms and their faces portray the great ordeal they had endured on the beaches in Dieppe. *National Archives of Canada PA 183775.*

These German soldiers are inspecting a trackless Churchill tank on the beach in Dieppe. Half of the Calgary Regiment's tanks successfully passed the beach, however, they were rapidly obliged to retreat to cover the fleeing infantrymen, before being abandoned. *National Archives of Canada - C 17293.*

Finally, the Allied strategists were henceforth convinced that a direct attack on a major port was impossible. The idea of developing artificial harbours for logistic purposes consequently emerged.

Nevertheless, to quote General Montgomery, "The price of this experience was truly excessive".

9

From left to right, the leading SHAEF Generals; seated, Air Chief Marshal Arthur Tedder (UK), Second in command, General Dwight Eisenhower "Ike" (USA), Commander in Chief, General Bernard Montgomery (UK), Commander of Ground Forces; standing, General Omar Bradley (USA), Commander of the US First Army, Admiral Bertram Ramsay (UK), in charge of naval forces, Air Chief Marshal Trafford Leigh Mallory (UK), in charge of air forces and General Walter Bedell-Smith (USA), Chief of Staff. *Rights reserved.*

OVERLORD AND THE 3RD CANADIAN DIVISION

During the Quadrant Conference held in Quebec in August 1943, the plan for Overlord, aimed at liberating North-West Europe, was approved by the Allied military chiefs. The plan, established by the British General Frederick Morgan's COSSAC (Chief of Staff to the Supreme Allied Commander), involved the landing of three divisions on the Calvados coastline in May 1944. The project for a landing operation in France dated back to 1940, however its development was hindered by conflicting strategic views among the Allied chiefs. The Americans were in favour of a direct attack in France, whereas Churchill preferred the idea of an invasion in the Balkans, Europe's "soft underbelly", to precede the Red Army. The American project was to prevail, in reason of the authority that had been progressively gained by the United States.

Late 1943, General Eisenhower was appointed Supreme Commander of the Allied Forces. His military staff, the SHAEF (Supreme Headquarters Allied Expeditionary Force) was established early 1944. Eisenhower and Montgomery, jointly in charge of Allied ground forces, were quick to realise that the COSSAC project was insufficient. Not only three, but five divisions were to land in Normandy, with additional support from three airborne divisions. This extension to the initial plan required an increased number of landing barges. Operation Overlord was consequently postponed for a month.

The 3rd Canadian Division
(Major-general Keller) 21,500 men

7th Brigade
(Brig. Foster)
1st wave of assault

The Royal Winnipeg Rifles
(Lt Col Meldram)

The Regina Rifle Regiment
(Lt Col Matheson)

1st Battalion, The Canadian Scottish Regiment
(Lt Col Cabeldu)

8th Brigade
(Brig. Blackader)
1st wave of assault

The Queen's Own Rifles of Canada
(Lt Col Spragge)

Le Régiment de la Chaudière
(Lt Col Mathieu)

The North Shore (New Brunswick) Regiment
(Lt Col Buell)

9th Brigade
(Brig. Cunningham)
Reinforcement brigade

The Highland Light Infantry of Canada
(Lt Col Griffiths)

The Stormont, Dundas and Glengarry Highlanders
(Lt Col Christiansen)

The North Nova Scotia Highlanders
(Lt Col Petch)

Divisional Units

4 artillery groups
(Ninety-six 105mm Priests)

1 anti-tank group
(Forty-eight 17-pounders)

1 anti-air group
(Fifty-four 40mm Bofors)

1 machine gun battalion
(The Cameron Highlanders of Ottawa (MG))

7th Reconnaissance Regiment
or
17th Duke of York's Royal Canadian Hussars

Attached unit: 2nd Canadian Armoured Brigade (Brigadier Wyman)

6th Armoured Regiment
or
1st Hussars
(Lt Col Colwell)

10th Armoured Regiment
or
Fort Garry Horse
(Lt Col Morton)

27th Armoured Regiment
or
The Sherbrooke Fusiliers Regiment
(Lt Col Gordon)

Other attached units

48th Royal Marine Commando (British) (Lt Col Moulton)

Crab anti-mine tanks: **Squadron B from the 22nd Dragoons and Squadron A from the Westminster Dragoons**

Other special tanks: **26th and 80th Squadrons from the 5th Assault Regiment, Royal Engineers**

Badges: *Juno Beach Centre/National Defense of Canada.*

The Canadians were scheduled to take part in the D-Day Landings as from the initial COSSAC plan. Major-general Keller was informed on the 3rd of July 1943 that his 3rd Division had been selected. Troop training was intensified, first of all in Scotland, near Inveraray, where copies of the German defences were built on the banks of Loch Lyne, then in the south of England, where the division was subjected to a number of coordination exercises with the RAF and the Royal Navy. Tanks from the attached 2nd Armoured Brigade also took part in these training exercises.

Allied cargo convoy in the Bedford Basin off Halifax in April 1942. *National Archives of Canada - PA 112993.*

Canadian soldiers in training in 1941. They adopted British equipment: uniform, battledress and weapons, Bren light machine gun, Lee-Enfield rifle and Thompson submachine gun. *National Archives of Canada - PA 132786.*

King George VI inspecting the 3rd Canadian Division's Priest self-propelled guns on the 25th of April 1944. These guns were to fire on the German coastal defences from their landing barges on the morning of the 6th of June. *National Archives of Canada - PA 145376.*

PREPARING FOR D-DAY

Late May, Keller's men were isolated in their camps in the vicinity of Southampton, along with other troops from General Crocker's British 1st Corps, scheduled to land to the east of the Allied attack. No contact with the outside world was allowed.

On the 2nd of June, they finally received the order to embark. Each and every one of them repeated the gestures they had rehearsed hundreds of times. But this was no longer a training exercise. A few days from then, they would find themselves on that Normandy beach, code named Juno.

Training for landing. Troops from the 3rd Division have just left HMCS *Prince Henry* to embark the LCA (Landing Craft Assault) landing barges that took them to the shore. *National Archives of Canada - PA 135889.*

13

PREPARING FOR D-DAY

THE ATLANTIC WALL ON JUNO BEACH

Stake surmounted with a mine, designed to explode under landing barges at high tide

As early as 1942, Hitler ordered for a series of fortifications to be built from Norway to the Spanish border, in order to prevent any Allied landing. However, the Atlantic Wall was far from an impenetrable fortification comparable to the Great Wall of China or Hadrian's Wall. It was in fact a series of resistance nests (*Widerstandsnest* or WN) dotted along the coastline and serving as mutual cover for each other. Each WN was equipped with one or several anti-tank guns and a series of small concrete fortifications to house machine guns and mortar. The approach to these WNs was protected by barbed wire and mines.

The Germans had also installed a number of defensive devices on the beaches; obstacles, tetrahedrons, Czech hedgehogs, mined stakes, the aim of which was to prevent any landing vessel from approaching the shorefront at high tide. And should the Allies opt for a low-tide landing, they would be obliged to cover several hundred metres under heavy fire from these German strong points. In reality, they were to partly overcome this problem by landing at mid tide.

Finally, the "Wall" comprised a third line of defence. Coastal artillery batteries were positioned here and there, either further inland or in ports, their aim being to sink ships from the Allied fleet. Some of them were in the form of concrete casemates, as in Pointe du Hoc or Longues-sur-Mer.

The Atlantic Wall was the subject of tremendous praise in German propaganda. However, the commanders on site were no fools. Field Marshal von Rundstedt, in charge of the 58 German divisions in the West, along with Field Marshal Rommel, in charge of the Army Group B, covering the coast from Brittany to the Netherlands, were both convinced that this "Wall" could resist but a few hours. The armoured divisions, the *Panzerdivisionen*, were to make the difference. However, the two German marshals had divergent opinions. Von Rundstedt was keen on the use of the Panzer divisions for vast counter-attacks over the days immediately following the landing, hence forcing the Allies back into the sea. On the contrary, Rommel believed that they should be used in the very first hours after the landing, to prevent the Allies from establishing a solid bridgehead. Finally, certain divisions were positioned within the vicinity of the beaches, such as the 21st *Panzer-Division* in Caen, others being placed further inland, such as the *Panzer-Lehr* in Chartres or the 12th SS "Hitlerjugend" in Évreux. This somewhat rough-and-ready solution was exacerbated by the fact that Hitler alone had the power to move these *Panzers*.

14

Bunker on the beach at Courseulles-sur-Mer housing an 88mm gun. Traces of Allied gunfire aimed at neutralising the weapon can be seen on the sides of the gun port.
National Archives of Canada - PA 140856.

Behind Juno Beach, on the eight kilometre stretch from Graye to Saint-Aubin, the sandy coastline was defended by the 736th Regiment's 2nd Battalion from General Richter's 716th Division. A few Osttruppen, Russians enlisted in the German Army, were also posted in the sector. The 2nd Battalion's companies, whose command post had been established in the fortified castle of Tailleville, were posted in the various WNs as follows:

LOCATION	STRONG POINT	WEAPONS	COMPANY
Saint-Aubin-sur-Mer	WN 27	One 50mm gun within a concrete shelter Machine guns and mortar	5th Company
Bernières-sur-Mer	WN 28	One 50mm gun within a concrete shelter One bunker surmounted by a tank turret Machine guns and mortar	
Courseulles-sur-Mer East of the River Seulles	WN 29	One 88mm gun within a casemate Two 75mm guns within a casemate Two 50mm guns Machine guns and mortar	6th Company
Village of Courseulles-sur-Mer	WN 30	Machine guns and mortar	
Courseulles-sur-Mer West of the River Seulles	WN 31	One 75mm gun within a casemate Two 50mm guns within a concrete shelter Machine guns and mortar	

Various artillery positions were established inland, however none of them were inside casemates. A vast radar station was set up in Douvres-la-Délivrande and Basly. The station's five radars were protected by a 200 man-strong garrison, sheltered in solid defensive positions.

Finally, a few armoured units from the 200th Assault Gun Battalion and the 21st *Panzer Division* were stationed in Le Fresne-Camilly and Villons-les-Buissons.

JUNO BEACH, A GATEWAY TO THE FORTRESS EUROPE

D-DAY ON JUNO BEACH

On the evening of the 5th of June, following a day's postponement due to poor weather conditions, Commodore Oliver's J Force cast off from ports in the vicinity of Southampton. A few hours later, the troops were due to land on Juno Beach. Aboard HMS *Hilary*, Commodore Oliver was in command of over 360 vessels of all sorts. They were accompanied by the naval bombardment E Force entrusted with the mission of destroying the coastal defences to facilitate Canadian progression. The E Force included HMS *Belfast* (twelve 152mm guns), HMS *Diadem* (eight 133mm guns) and 11 destroyers, one of them French, La *Combattante* belonging to the FNFL (*Forces Navales de la France Libre*) and two of them Canadian, the SIOUX and the ALGONQUIN. All of these ships were soon to join the 7,000 other vessels assembled at Piccadilly Circus, an assembly point off the Isle of Wight. They then separated in the form of five distinct forces and headed for the five predetermined landing zones: the Americans on Utah and Omaha, the British and Canadians on Gold, Juno and Sword.

Canadian paratroopers

In the SHAEF plan, airborne divisions were to cover the flanks of the amphibious assault. The zone between the Rivers Orne and Dives, to the east, was to be secured by the British 6th Airborne Division. Within this unit, Lieutenant Colonel Bradbrooke's 1st Canadian Battalion had been entrusted with the mission of destroying the bridges at Varaville and Robehomme. Despite their great dispersion on landing, the Canadian paratroopers successfully accomplished their mission.

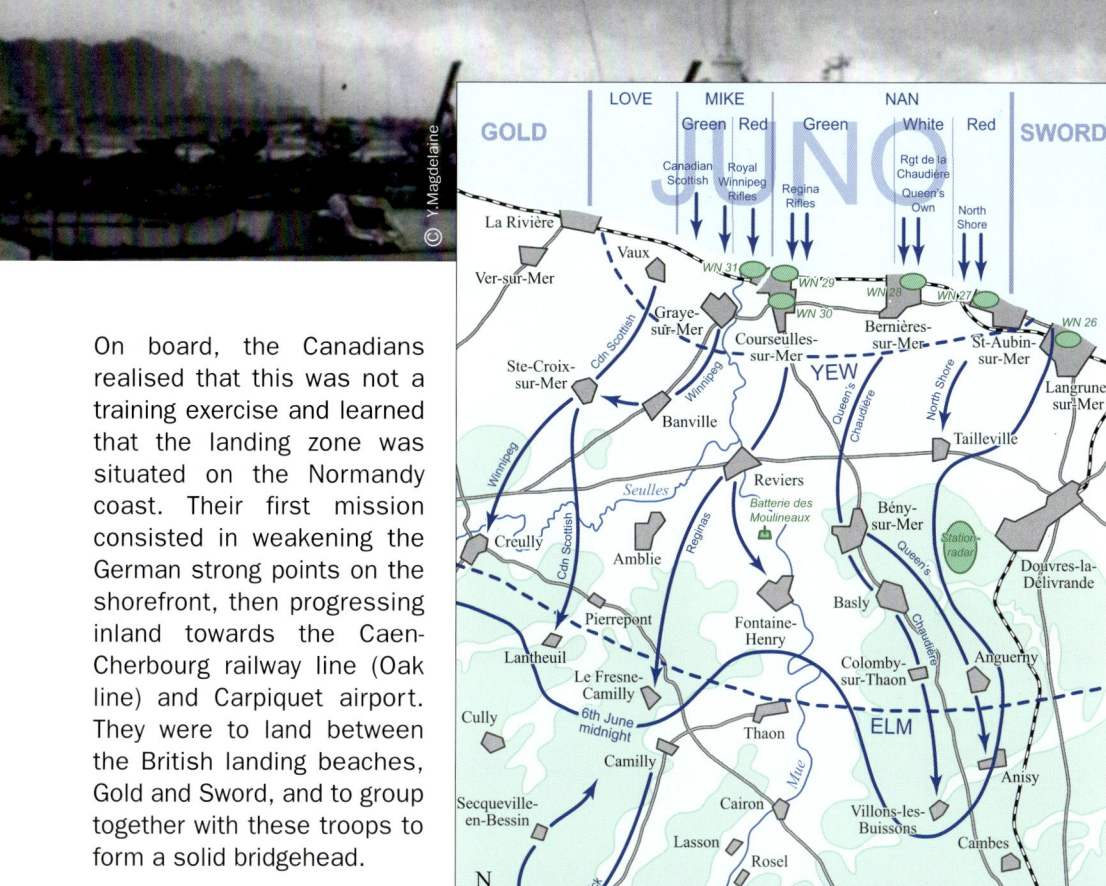

On board, the Canadians realised that this was not a training exercise and learned that the landing zone was situated on the Normandy coast. Their first mission consisted in weakening the German strong points on the shorefront, then progressing inland towards the Caen-Cherbourg railway line (Oak line) and Carpiquet airport. They were to land between the British landing beaches, Gold and Sword, and to group together with these troops to form a solid bridgehead.

At 05:00 hours, the ships anchored 12 kilometres from the coast. The German defences had already been bombarded around midnight by RAF and RCAF (Royal Canadian Air Force) planes, then at dawn by heavy bombers from the 8th US Air Force. Unfortunately, most of the bombs had missed their targets, falling further inland due to poor visibility caused by bad weather conditions. Naval bombing then took over, whilst troops left their ships to board small LCA (Landing Craft Assault) landing barges.

H-Hour (07:40) was scheduled ten minutes after the British landing because of a reef situated off Juno Beach, in order to avoid the barges from grounding or being ripped open on the rocks. However, the sea was particularly choppy, with one-metre-high waves, hence leading to a further delay of ten to fifteen minutes. Consequently, the obstacles on the beach were covered by the tide to a greater extent than planned and around a third of these small Canadian barges were lost in the incessant ebb and flow.

Paratroopers from the 1st Canadian Parachute Battalion in a transit camp in Britain, a few days before D-Day.
National Archives of Canada - PA 114588.

After the landing operation, the beach at Saint-Aubin-sur-Mer was scattered with debris of all sorts. In particular, the skeleton of a Sherman DD tank and an American P-47 Thunderbolt whose journey had come to a tragic end. *USAF - 72625 AC.*

The attack on the beach had been rehearsed over and over again. The first approach was to be made by the Sherman Duplex Drive amphibious tanks, launched over three kilometres from the coast. Once their inflatable skirts had been folded away, they were to attack the German defences. Later, AVRE (Assault Vehicle Royal Engineers) tanks, anti-mine tanks, bridge building tanks… were to free the way for the infantrymen aboard the LCA landing craft.

The coast was approaching. The Canadians could finally distinguish the landmarks they had been given during training. Behind them, the LCTR rockets intensified bombing on the beaches, with additional help from the 105mm guns aboard self-propelled Priests loaded onto LCTs (Landing Craft Tank). Rockets and shells whizzed above the infantry landing barges, somewhat reassuring the men onboard. But who could survive such a deluge of gun-fire? Unfortunately, they were quick to realise that very few German defences had actually been struck by these successive bombings.

Shells and mortar began to shower the barges. Machine gun bullets riddled their metallic superstructure. Certain barges struck the mined stakes, exploded and began to sink. Their ramps were then lowered, and the frenetic race towards the shore began.

Aerial view of the Mike Red sector. The meande River Seulles can clearly be seen.
Courtesy of the Laurier Centre for Military Strategic Disarmament Studies.

7:49 The Royal Winnipeg Rifles land to the west of the River Seulles

The B Company arrived in the Mike Red sector immediately opposite the defences of WN 31 to meet with a bloodbath. None of the amphibious tanks was on the beach. The rough seas had delayed their launch. Two thirds of the company were rapidly put out of action. The situation was only to improve upon the arrival of seven Sherman DDs belonging to the 1st Hussars. The German position was finally cleared and the capture of an intact bridge over the Seulles offered a progression route inland.

Further west, on Mike Green sector, the D Company was more fortunate. Barely hit by German defensive fire, the company rapidly advanced towards Graye. Specially equipped tanks ensured the passage over the marshy area immediately behind the beach.

JUNO BEACH, A GATEWAY TO THE FORTRESS EUROPE
D-Day on Juno Beach

However, one of them was to remain there for many years (see picture).

At the western extremity of Mike Green, the C Company from the 1st Canadian Scottish Regiment also met with little resistance. Its primary aim, a casemate housing a 75mm anti-tank gun, had already been neutralised by naval bombardments.

The Canadians then moved on to the Château de Vaux where they drove out a few Russian defenders from the 441st East Battalion.

Juno Beach Centre.

When crossing the marshy zone to the west of the River Seulles, this Churchill Petard got stuck in a crater it was supposed to fill with fascines. The tank belonged to a unit from General Hobart's 79th Armoured Division. This quite distinctive division was equipped with a number of tanks designed to facilitate progression across the beaches and beyond the German defences. Anti-mine, bridge building, fascine or bunker destroyer tanks were all part of Hobart's "menagerie". For D-Day, the division did not fight as an independent unit, but loaned its tanks to the three British-Canadian divisions that landed.

In fact, this Churchill Petard was itself covered with fascines, then the Engineers filled the crater to build a road. It was finally dislodged in 1976 to become a commemorative monument.

8:00 **Le *North Shore* (*New Brunswick*) Regiment in Saint-Aubin**

Whilst the A Company met with feeble resistance to the west of Saint-Aubin, the B Company fell face to face with WN 27 and found itself trapped against the sea wall. Once more, the Sherman DDs were behind schedule and the infantrymen had to fend for themselves. As the armoured vehicles arrived, they were rapidly in the firing line of anti-tank weapons. However, both troops and special tanks finally managed to penetrate as far as the streets of Saint-Aubin to attack the German positions from the rear. Nevertheless, it took a good few hours before the North Shore Regiment had cleared the village of its last snipers. Saint-Aubin was totally under Allied control the following day.

SUR CETTE PLAGE DE SAINT-AUBIN, A L'AUBE DU 6 JUIN 1944, A 7H30 FUT ETABLIE UNE TÊTE DE PONT PAR LE RÉGIMENT D'INFANTERIE CANADIENNE DES "NORTH SHORE", OUVRANT LA VOIE AU 48 ÈME COMMANDO DES "ROYAL MARINES"

Commemorative plaque on Saint-Aubin beach, paying tribute to the village's liberators.
Juno Beach Centre.

19

D-Day, Canadian vehicles travelling through Courseulles-sur-Mer. Their aim: the Caen-Cherbourg railway line.
National Archives of Canada - PA 130159.

At 08:45, the time had come for the British troops from the 48th Royal Marine Commando to arrive. Two of their six landing barges hit mined stakes and sunk, resulting in heavy losses before the landing itself. The commandos, whose mission was to join forces with their counterparts on Sword Beach, remained trapped at the sea wall. The improved situation in the village eventually enabled them to advance towards Langrune with two Centaur tanks. However, the German positions proved too powerful for the 48th Commando, which lost half of its men. The liaison with Sword Beach was not to be made on D-Day as initially planned.

This 50mm gun housed within a casemate on Saint-Aubin beach was to prove a tenacious hurdle for the North Shore Regiment, before finally being neutralised. *Courtesy of the Laurier Centre for Military Strategic and Disarmament Studies.*

8:05 The Regina Rifles attack WN 29 in Courseulles

The A Company was the first to land in the Nan Green sector. It was to challenge WN 29, a powerful defensive complex comprising several concrete shelters. When the Regina Rifles landed, fourteen Sherman DD tanks were already geared up on the beach. Although four armoured vehicles had been lost in the rough seas, none of the surviving fourteen tanks was destroyed during their duel with the WN 29's anti-tank guns. The arrival of special tanks was to seal the fate of these coastal defences and to free the way towards the village of Courseulles which had been divided into twelve sectors (blocks). The first blocks were already secured. However, the tide was rising and when C and D companies

JUNO BEACH, A GATEWAY TO THE FORTRESS EUROPE
D-Day on Juno Beach

arrived, several of their barges exploded on the mined obstacles, no longer visible on the beach. Nevertheless, thanks to these reinforcements, the Regina Rifles had gained total control of Courseulles by 10:00 hours. Lieutenant Colonel Matheson then began to group together his men for their southward advance.

However, firing resumed from the beach defences. The Germans had taken advantage of a network of subterranean galleries to withdraw, before resurfacing and reoccupying their positions. Two hours of relentless combat were required to finally defeat them.

Courseulles: this small fishing village was used as an unloading and resupplying port. Twelve old ships were wrecked off Courseulles to form one of the five Gooseberries to be developed along the Normandy coastline. These old ships served as a breakwater, hence facilitating the unloading of supplies on the beaches. As from the 8th of June, some 2,000 tonnes were shipped to Courseulles daily.

Juno Beach Centre.

The "Bold": This tank, now displayed on the Place du 6 Juin, is a Sherman Duplex Drive that belonged to the 1st Hussars. (Duplex Drive, because the tank's engine powered, not only the tracks, but also propellers located to the rear of the vehicle). Equipped with an inflatable skirt that rose above the turret, these DDs were launched over three kilometres off the coast before making their own way to the shore. Once on the beach, the skirt was deflated and the tank could then set to attacking the German defences. However, the Bold never reached the beach. It was dragged out of the water in 1971, under the impetus of Léo Gariépy, a French-speaking Canadian who had landed in Courseulles on the 6th of June with his DD tank and who settled in the village after the war.

8:05 The Queen's Own Rifles of Canada struggle in Bernières

In Bernières, the scenario was the same as for the other beaches. Certain units landed without encountering major difficulty, whilst others suffered heavy losses. The B Company drifted 200 metres off-course to land directly opposite WN 28. The men bravely thrust forward, but a third of them never left the beach. Others remained trapped behind the highly distinctive breakwater, still in place today.

The DD tanks were behind schedule. Due to the extremely rough seas, their commander had decided to unload them directly on the beach. An audacious feat by Lieutenant Herbert, Corporal Tessier and Private Chicoski, closely followed by their fellow troops, using grenades and Sten submachine guns, was to secure the capture of the German strong point. The A company landed further westwards, suffering fewer losses.

D-Day, the streets of Courseulles-sur-Mer became quickly congested with all sorts of vehicles, including, in the forefront, this DUKW, an amphibious Allied vehicle. *National Archives of Canada - PA 132464.*

Canadian soldier watching over German prisoners behind the breakwater on the beach at Bernières.
National Archives of Canada - PA 133154.

At 08:30, the *Régiment de la Chaudière* started to land. Once more, the tide had risen and the obstacles on the beach were barely visible. Mines sunk many barges, leading to great losses, many other Canadians wading their way to the shore up to their chests in water.

At 09:00 hours, special tanks and DDs finally landed and Bernières was cleared of its remaining defenders. The *Régiment de la Chaudière* was then free to parade through the village, much to the surprise of its inhabitants, astonished to hear them speaking French. Continuous reinforcements flowed in, however the small and winding streets of Bernières were far from suitable for such a throng of vehicles and men. The situation was exacerbated when Major-general Keller, unaware of the difficult conditions in the village, also ordered his reserve troops from the 9th Brigade to land in Bernières. Massive traffic jams in the small coastal village were to seriously hinder any inland advance.

The distinctive form of a DUKW in front of a typical Norman villa. This type of amphibious truck had proved to be a valuable asset for the Allies, transporting thousands of tons of supplies from ship to shore. *Canadian Forces Joint Imagery Centre.*

▲ An MP (Military Police) searching a German prisoner's pockets. *Canadian Forces Joint Imagery Centre.*

A stone's throw from the station in Bernières-sur-Mer, a ▲ soldier from the *Régiment de la Chaudière* having fun with a young local. *Canadian Forces Joint Imagery Centre.*

JUNO BEACH, A GATEWAY TO THE FORTRESS EUROPE

INLAND PROGRESSION

As from 10:00 hours, the first line (Yew) was virtually in reach. German defences were either totally neutralised or close to being so, and the coastal villages were now clear. At this point, the objective was to regroup troops and to coordinate progression inland. To the west, the 1st Canadian Scottish and the Royal Winnipeg Rifles quickly made their way to Sainte-Croix and Banville. With support from the 1st Hussars' tanks, they overturned the German resistance nests and reached Creully, where they joined forces with units from the British 50th Division that had landed on Gold Beach. Together, they advanced to Pierrepont where they settled for the night.

After having cleared Courseulles, the Regina Rifles reached Reviers at 11:00 hours. By dusk, they had advanced to Fontaine-Henry and Le Fresne-Camilly. On their way, they had overcome a German position, whose 88mm gun had succeeded in destroying six Sherman tanks. Lieutenant McCormick from the 1st Hussars' C Squadron moved even further inland to observe the Carpiquet airfield. Although there were no enemy troops in the sector, he decided to withdraw to Le Fresne-Camilly for fear of isolating, hence jeopardising his unit.

With the Bernières jams now behind them, the Queen's Own Rifles and the Régiment de la Chaudière advanced towards Bény. A further German position was overwhelmed thanks to the Fort Garry Horse Regiment's Sherman tanks, followed by an assault on the Les Moulineaux artillery battery equipped with a 100mm gun. By evening, the Canadians had taken control of Anguerny and Villons-les-Buissons, some 12 kilometres from the coast.

▲ The Canadians continued to land relentlessly throughout the day – ▲
a total of 21,500 were operational by the evening of D-Day.
Canadian Forces Joint Imagery Centre.

The North Shore finally triumphed over Saint-Aubin to advance towards the *Château de Tailleville*, where the 2nd Battalion from the German 716th Division's 736th Regiment had set up its command post. The castle walls had been reinforced by a series of bunkers, however, armoured vehicles from the Fort Garry Horse's C Squadron successfully defeated the position. However it was too late to attack the nearby radar station in Douvres.

Major-general Keller could quite rightly be proud of the day's results. The landing was deemed a success, even if the Oak line, the Caen-Cherbourg railway, had not yet been reached. A total of 21,500 men had landed with over 3,000 vehicles and some 2,500 tonnes of military material. Losses were in fact half of the Allies' estimated 2,000. 359 Canadians lost their lives. A further 650 were wounded.

Juno Beach and its famous visitors

Over the days that followed the landings, Juno was to welcome several illustrious figures. The first was the British Prime Minister, Winston Churchill, who arrived in Courseulles on the 12th of June. He also paid a visit to General Montgomery in his headquarters in Creullet. Two days later, the French President, General de Gaulle landed near Courseulles. It was the first time he had set foot on French soil for four years. An 18-metre-high Cross of Lorraine was erected on this historic spot in 1990. De Gaulle then travelled to Bayeux, where he was given a triumphal welcome. Finally, King George VI in turn landed in Courseulles on the 16th of June.

Rights reserved.

Troops from the 3rd Division leaving their LCI (Landing Craft Infantry) barge on the beach at Bernières. The tide was already high and the mass of vehicles crowded the narrow strip of sand. Inland progression was imminent.
National Archives of Canada - PA 131506.

JUNO BEACH, A GATEWAY TO THE FORTRESS EUROPE

PROGRESSIVE DISILLUSIONMENT

On the morning of the 7th of June, Canadian troops from the 3rd Division continued their progression following in Lieutenant McCormick's footsteps. However, reinforcements from the 12th Panzer Division "Hilterjugend" were quick to arrive in the sector. These young and fanatical Hitlerian recruits, hence their division's name, set up position to the west of Caen and succeeded in hindering the town's liberation for over a month. Several Canadian soldiers were captured by the SS during fighting around the villages of Putot-en-Bessin, Authie and Buron. Twenty-seven of them were executed in the gardens of Ardenne Abbey, where Colonel Kurt Meyer from the 25th *Panzergrenadier* Regiment had set up his command post. A further 26 were slain in the grounds of the Château de Pavie in Audrieu, and 35 on the road to Fontenay-le-Pesnel.

After a month of violent conflict, the Canadians resumed their assault on Carpiquet airfield (Operation Windsor) on the 4th of July; however, once more, the operation failed to overwhelm the SS defences. Five days later, the Canadian and British troops joined forces for Operation Charnwood, aimed at finally liberating Caen. The German defences were crushed at last, thanks to strategic bombing and the Canadian and British troops triumphed on the banks of the River Orne on the afternoon of the 9th of July amidst a town reduced to ruins. However, Caen's right bank was still under German control.

🪂 Droping zone for the 1st Canadian Parachute Battalion on 6th June
SPRING Allied operations involving Canadian participation   💥 Canadian combat zone

© Y.Magdelaine   The Canadians in the Battle of Normandy.

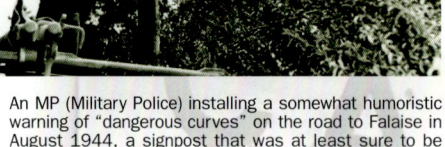

An MP (Military Police) installing a somewhat humoristic warning of "dangerous curves" on the road to Falaise in August 1944, a signpost that was at least sure to be noticed by passing motorists.
National Archives of Canada - PA 131272.

A new assault, code named Operation Goodwood, was then launched. The aim was to bypass Caen from the east. Concurrently, General Simonds' 2nd Canadian Corps was to cross the Orne and continue southwards (Operation Atlantic). The 2nd Corps had been operational since the 11th of July. It was in charge, not only of the 3rd Canadian Division, in action since the 6th of June, but also General Foulkes' 2nd Canadian Division which was preparing to fight for the very first time in Normandy.

The Canadians successfully crossed the River Orne to liberate the south bank, however they were stopped in their tracks by German defences on the Verrières Ridge. Even after six weeks of relentless combat, the German front remained steadfast. The overall situation was, however, to the Allies' advantage. A total of 1,500,000 men were now in position throughout Normandy and the German forces were on their knees. The Allied deception operation, code named Fortitude, had surpassed their expectations. Several German divisions were requisitioned and geared up in the Pas-de-Calais, for the enemy command remained convinced that a landing operation was imminent.

Mealtime for men from the Stormont Dundas and Glengarry Highlanders Regiment on the railway platform in Caen in August 1944.
Conseil Régional de Basse-Normandie
National Archives of Canada.

A concentration of Sherman tanks from the Fort Garry Horse Regiment – 2nd Canadian Armoured Brigade, near Bretteville-le-Rabet on the 14th of August. They are preparing for Operation Tractable, aimed at liberating Falaise. *National Archives of Canada PA 113658.*

JUNO BEACH, A GATEWAY TO THE FORTRESS EUROPE
Progressive disillusionment

On the 25th of July, the Americans broke through the front to the west of Saint-Lô (Operation Cobra). General Bradley's men achieved a 60 kilometre advance to enter Brittany in just one week. Simultaneously, General Montgomery launched Operation Spring, entrusted to General Crerar's 1st Canadian Army and aimed at sustaining pressure on the German defences in the Caen plain. The 2nd Canadian Division was given the mission of capturing the Verrières Ridge from either side of the Falaise road. However, the sector was propitious to the enemy, for riddled with former iron ore galleries which they used to attack the Canadians from the rear. Bitter combat, all day long, only offered but a meagre advance. The operation was suspended at dusk. The 25th of July 1944 was undoubtedly one of the cruellest dates in the Canadian Army's history. A total of 1,500 men were killed, wounded or lost. Early August, whilst the Americans were liberating Brittany and Anjou, the British and Canadian troops remained at a standstill to the south of Caen: they had advanced but 25 kilometres in two months. Montgomery was eager to penetrate towards Falaise, a mission he entrusted to General Simonds' 2nd Canadian Corps. Two consecutive attacks (Operation Totalize and Operation Tractable) were to prove necessary before the men from the 2nd Canadian troops could enter Falaise on the 16th of August.

The town of Caen endured over a month of bitter combat. It was only on the 9th of July that Canadian and British troops finally freed the town, by then virtually razed to the ground. These soldiers are walking through the ruins in Rue Saint-Pierre. In the background, what remained of the tower of the eponymous church. *National Archives of Canada - PA 116510.*

Major Currie. *Courtesy of the Laurier Centre for Military Strategic and Disarmament Studies.*

Victoria Cross.

By now the Germans had been forced into total retreat for fear of being trapped between the Americans in Argentan and the Canadians in Falaise. Their only possible escape was via a narrow passageway, barely ten kilometres wide, in the vicinity of Chambois. The 2nd Canadian Corps' two armoured divisions, the 4th Canadian Armoured Division and the 1st Polish Armoured Division, were sent to close the gap. On the 19th of August, Major Currie from the South Alberta Regiment (4th Canadian Armoured Division) arrived in Saint-Lambert-sur-Dive. Currie maintained his position and took hundreds of German prisoners, despite several counter-attacks. He was later to be awarded the highest Commonwealth military decoration for valour, the Victoria Cross.

Finally, late August, the Allied target became the River Seine, in the vicinity of Rouen, following fierce combat in La Londe Forest.

On the 19th of August, Major Currie's South Alberta Regiment took control of part of Saint-Lambert-sur-Dive, with support from the Sutherland Highlanders. His regiment took over 2,000 German prisoners during their attempted flight from the Falaise pocket. *National Archives of Canada - PA 111565.*

JUNO BEACH, A GATEWAY TO THE FORTRESS EUROPE

These two solders from the 2nd Canadian Division are enjoying a moment's respite on the edge of the fountain in Falaise's Place Saint-Gervais. On the left, a motorcyclist, recognisable thanks to his helmet and high boots. *Courtesy of the Laurier Centre for Military Strategic and Disarmament Studies.*

❶ - All of the 1st Canadian Army chiefs in May 1945 in The Netherlands: from left to right, seated: Generals Maczek (1st Polish Armoured Division), Simonds (2nd Canadian Corps), Crerar (First Canadian Army), Foulkes (1st Canadian Corps), Hoffmeister (5th Armoured Division); standing: Generals Keefler (3rd Division), Matthews (2nd Division), Foster (1st Division), Moncel (4th Armoured Brigade) and Rawlings (British 49th Division).
National Archives of Canada - PA 137473.

THE LIBERATION OF THE REST OF EUROPE

In the early days of September, the Canadian divisions from General Crerar's First Army cleared the Channel coast. The 2nd Division was entrusted with the honour of liberating Dieppe two years after the tragic events of 1942. They then continued to pursue the German troops throughout Belgium. In the autumn of 1944, Field Marshal Model successfully established a continuous front on the border with the Reich.

Despite the liberation of Antwerp, the Germans were entrenched in their positions north of the mouth of the Scheldt, preventing any access to Belgian ports. However, in October, they were taken by assault by Canadian troops, backed up by commandos. Winter came, and the Americans resisted a German counter-attack in the Ardennes further south.

Progression was resumed in February 1945. The Canadians were then entrusted with a mission code named Operation Veritable, consisting in clearing the left bank of the Rhine in the region of Reichswald. Combat proved to be extremely tough in this vast and flooded zone. Then, in April, they were ready to cross the Rhine, liberate The Netherlands and enter Germany, via the North Sea coast.

Men from the 2nd Canadian Division being offered a warm welcome by the inhabitants of Rouen; the cathedral can be seen in the background. The town suffered heavy Allied bombing, in particular on the banks of the Seine where hundreds of German vehicles converged in an attempt to cross the river and retreat.
National Archives of Canada - PA 131346.

❷ - The 2nd Canadian Division was entrusted with the honour of liberating Dieppe on the 1st of September 1944, two years after the tragedy of Operation Jubilee in which the division had taken part. Two days later, they proudly paraded before their commander, General Foulkes, together with General Crerar, commander of the First Canadian Army.
National Archives of Canada - PA 167562.

JUNO BEACH, A GATEWAY TO THE FORTRESS EUROPE

❸ - KAPUT, the Germans were indeed kaput as quoted in the headlines of the Canadian forces' newspaper, the "Maple Leaf". News that was, of course, to delight these men from the 12th Artillery Regiment.

JUNO BEACH TODAY

If you take a stroll along Juno Beach today, you will still see a few remaining vestiges of the battle that was to oppose thousands of men. The only attack now suffered by the bunkers along the beach is that of the sea spray. Two tanks, a Churchill Petard and the "Bold", a Sherman Duplex Drive in Courseulles, bear witness to the vital role played by such special vehicles in the success of the D-Day Landings. Many commemorative monuments also pay tribute to the great sacrifice made by battalions from the 3rd Canadian Division.

Further inland, in Bény-sur-Mer/Reviers and Cintheaux/Bretteville-sur-Laize, you will find two military cemeteries where most of the 5,500 Canadians who lay down their lives to liberate Normandy are now laid to rest.

Normans laying flowers on the grave of a Canadian soldier from a Scottish regiment, recognisable thanks to the Glengarry on the cross.
National Archives of Canada - PA 107940.

Juno Beach Centre / Terry Bond.